·HIDDEN WORLDS·
HEATHER AMERY·JANE SONGI

THE HUMAN
BODY

·HIDDEN WORLDS·
HEATHER AMERY·JANE SONGI

THE HUMAN
BODY

MARVELS THROUGH THE MICROSCOPE

HAMLYN

Editor: Julia Gorton
Designer: Hugh Schermuly
Picture Researcher: Emily Hedges
Production Controller: Ruth Charlton

First published in 1993 by Hamlyn Children's Books,
an imprint of Reed International Books Limited,
Michelin House, 81 Fulham Road, London SW3 6RB,
and Auckland, Melbourne, Singapore and Toronto.

This paperback edition published in 1994.

ISBN 0 600 58430 5

Cataloguing-in-Publication Data.
A catalogue record for this book is available from the British Library.

Printed in Italy

CONTENTS

Introduction 4

At Your Fingertips 6

Under Your Skin 8

Hairs by the Hundreds 10

Cutting Back 12

A Question of Taste 14

Vital Vision 16

Playing by Ear 18

Life Support 20

    Taking Air 22

    Food Factory 24

    All in the Blood 26

    Getting the Message 28

    A New Life 30

    Body at War 32

People Pests 34

Guess What? 36

Glossary 37

Index 38

Acknowledgements 40

INTRODUCTION

When you look closely, you can see all sorts of small things - a grain of sugar, a tiny insect or a speck of dust. With a magnifying glass, which is a glass lens, you can see much more detail.

Microscopes, which have several glass lenses, were invented nearly 400 years ago. For the first time, scientists could see the germs which cause disease, the countless cells in our blood, and millions of other things that no-one knew existed. Microscopes today can magnify an object up to 2,000 times its normal size.

We can now look even closer with electron microscopes, which were invented about 60 years ago. Instead of light, these microscopes use a beam of electrons to "look" at tiny things, and can magnify up to 250,000 times.

This researcher is using a scanning electron microscope to examine a tiny object. The pictures show up on a television screen.

This technician is using a light microscope to study samples of bacteria.

Sugar as we usually see it.

Magnified 2.5 times, a collection of glass-like crystals.

At 50 times their normal size, are these crystals or boulders?

This is how the corner of one crystal looks when it is magnified 500 times.

4

THE HUMAN
BODY

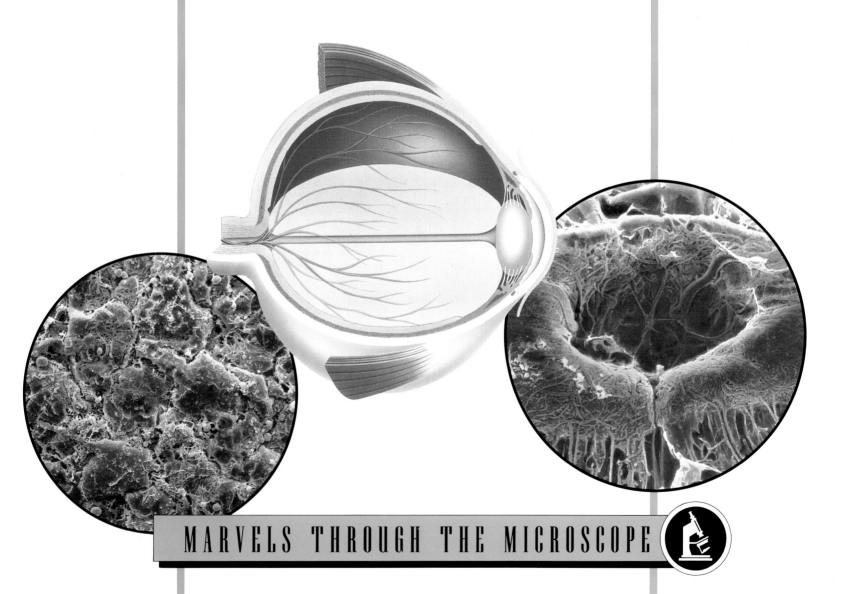

At Your Fingertips

Surface of nail
(x 300)

Touching, carrying, catching, drawing - how could you do any of these things without your hands? Hands are one of the most sensitive parts of your body. This is because there are masses of nerve endings in them which send messages to your brain. You can feel rough and smooth things with your fingertips as well as heat and cold. The skin of your palms is very tough. It is thicker here than anywhere else on your body, except the soles of your feet.

Personal prints

On the skin on the ends of your fingers and thumbs are patterns of small circles and loops. These are your fingerprints and yours are different from almost every-one else's. The chances of two people having the same prints is about one to 64,000 million. You can take your own finger-prints by dabbing ink or paint on your fingers and thumbs and pressing them on to paper.

Fingerprint

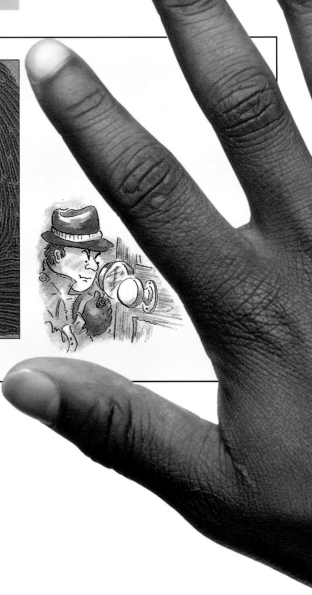

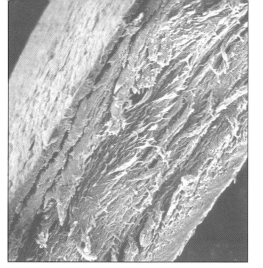

Tough as nails (left). Your nails are made of a tough substance called keratin. This is the same substance which makes your hair. The part of your nail which grows out of your skin is dead. That is why it doesn't hurt when you cut your nails. Nails are growing very slowly all the time, at a rate of about 2mm a month. It takes about six months to grow a whole new nail.

End of nail
(x 100)

Your nails make the ends of your fingers, and your toes, firm and tough. The nails protect them from knocks and blows which could hurt and damage the ends. The half moons on your nails look white because the nails are not firmly joined to the skin underneath.

Little flakes fall and are rubbed off our skin all the time. During our lives, each of us sheds about 18kg of skin.

Man's palm
(x 35)

Flakes of skin
(x 60)

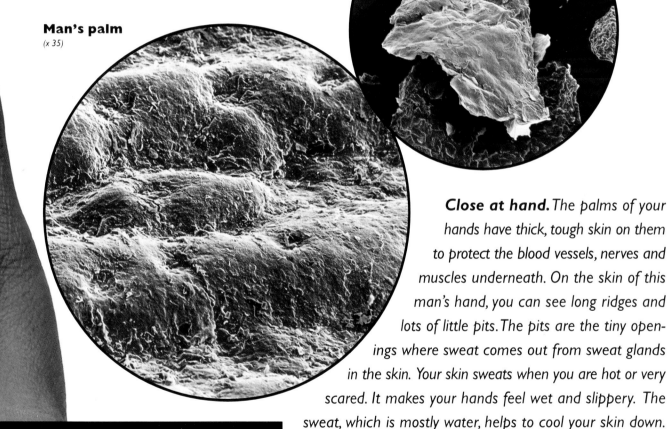

Close at hand. The palms of your hands have thick, tough skin on them to protect the blood vessels, nerves and muscles underneath. On the skin of this man's hand, you can see long ridges and lots of little pits. The pits are the tiny openings where sweat comes out from sweat glands in the skin. Your skin sweats when you are hot or very scared. It makes your hands feel wet and slippery. The sweat, which is mostly water, helps to cool your skin down.

An Indian man had a thumb nail which was 117cm long - over three times the height of this page.

Under Your Skin

A tailor-made waterproof, a tough, protective cushion, a barrier against disease-carrying germs - your skin is all these things and much more. It also works as a kind of thermostat, helping to keep you at the right temperature. Skin can even make one of the vitamins we need to stay healthy (vitamin D) if there is enough sunlight.

Skin deep (below)*. Under the top layer of your skin are masses of tiny blood vessels and nerve endings. The blood vessels help to give the skin its colour. When you are hot, they grow bigger, letting more blood through. This helps you to lose heat from your body and makes you look red. When you are cold, the blood vessels grow smaller and reduce the amount of blood in them. This makes you look pale. It also stops you losing heat from your body. The nerve endings are sensitive to heat, cold, touch, pressure and pain. Pain helps to keep your body healthy by telling you about injuries and when some part of your body is not well.*

Hair on skin
(x 725)

DID YOU KNOW?

On a warm day, a man loses about 1 litre of sweat a day. On a very hot day, he may lose up to 7 litres of sweat, enough to fill a bucket. This makes him very thirsty and he should eat extra salt to make up for the salt lost in the sweat.

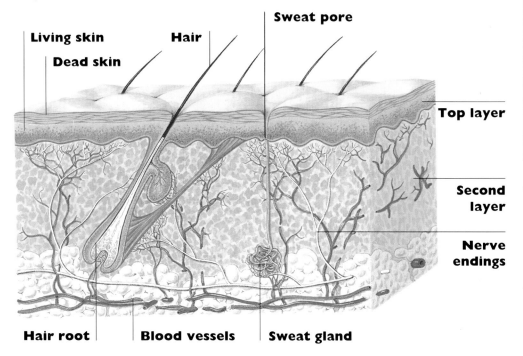

Living skin

Dead skin

Hair

Sweat pore

Top layer

Second layer

Nerve endings

Hair root

Blood vessels

Sweat gland

There are two main layers of skin. The top layer sheds flakes of old, dead skin while new skin grows underneath. In the second layer are sweat and oil glands, as well as the roots of hair and nails.

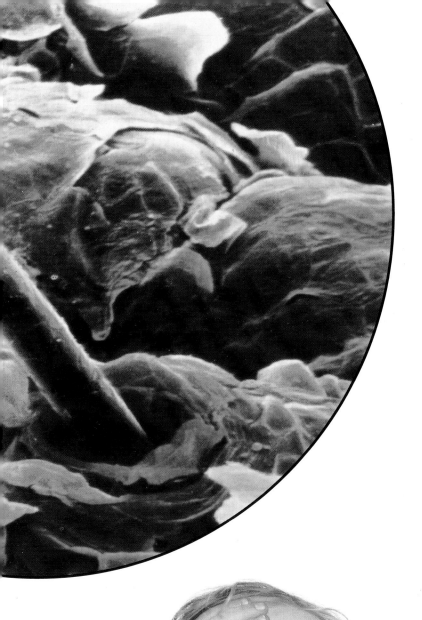

Hair grows out of tiny tubes in your skin. At the bottom of each tube are tiny cells which put the colour into hair. White hair is not really white. It is hair which is transparent and has no colour at all.

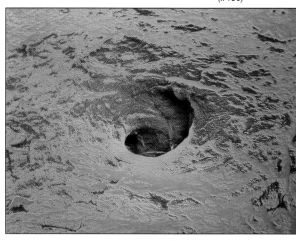

(x 150)

Sweat pores in skin

(x 260)

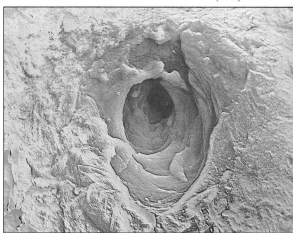

Cool it. Sweat helps to cool your body down and stops your temperature from going up. When you get very hot, it comes out of glands in your skin, through the pores, and dries on the surface. It takes heat from your skin as it dries and makes you feel cooler. This cooling system does not work well if the air around you is very damp, even if it is hot. This is because the sweat cannot dry quickly on your skin. Some people sweat a lot when they are playing games or are frightened. Then they often sweat most from the palms of their hands and soles of their feet where there are many sweat pores in their skin. Sweat is mostly water with a little salt and other chemicals in it.

Hairs by the Hundreds

Hair grows out of the skin on almost every part of your body. The only places where you don't have any at all are on your lips, the palms of your hands, the soles of your feet, and the sides and tips of your fingers and toes. Some of your hair is thick and you can easily see and feel it. Some is so fine and short that you can't see it unless you look very closely. Altogether, you have about 5 million hairs on your body which are growing and falling off all the time.

New hairs
(x 185)

Three-year cycle. *Each hair on a person's head grows for about three years before falling out. If hair is not cut regularly or is often bleached to make it blonde or dyed to change the colour, the ends of the hair become unhealthy and frayed. The end of this hair (left) is ragged and split.*

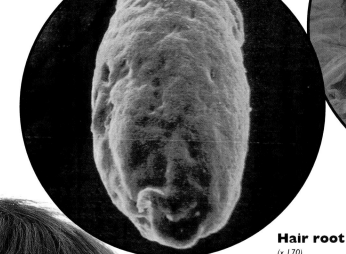

Hair root
(x 170)

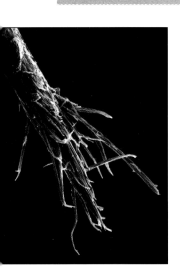

Split hair end
(x 400)

Most people have between 100,000 and 200,000 hairs on their heads.

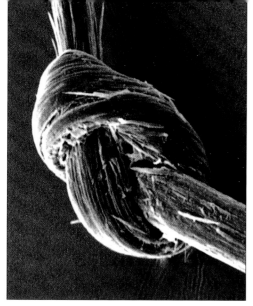

Knotted hair
(x 300)

If a hair is tied into tiny knots, the strand is damaged. The hair surface becomes rough, with short pieces breaking off.

Normal, healthy hair has long, smooth strands. Each hair is hollow with a coating of smooth scales. They are made of a tough material called keratin, which also makes your nails.

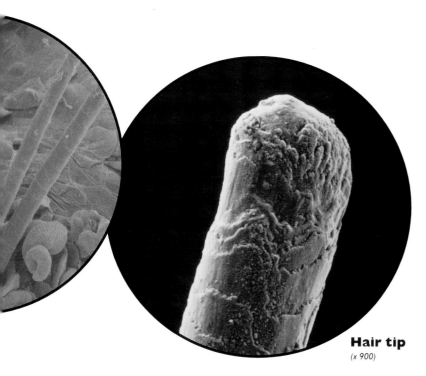

Hair tip
(x 900)

Pushing through the skin. The three hairs shown in the centre are growing out of someone's head. The short, fat one is new. The two thinner ones are older. Each hair grows out of a tiny tube in the skin. It has a root under the skin and a very small gland which supplies the hair with oil to make it smooth and glossy. It also has a tiny muscle which pulls the hair upright when someone is scared or cold and makes their hair "stand on end".

Normal hair
(x 475)

Cutting Back

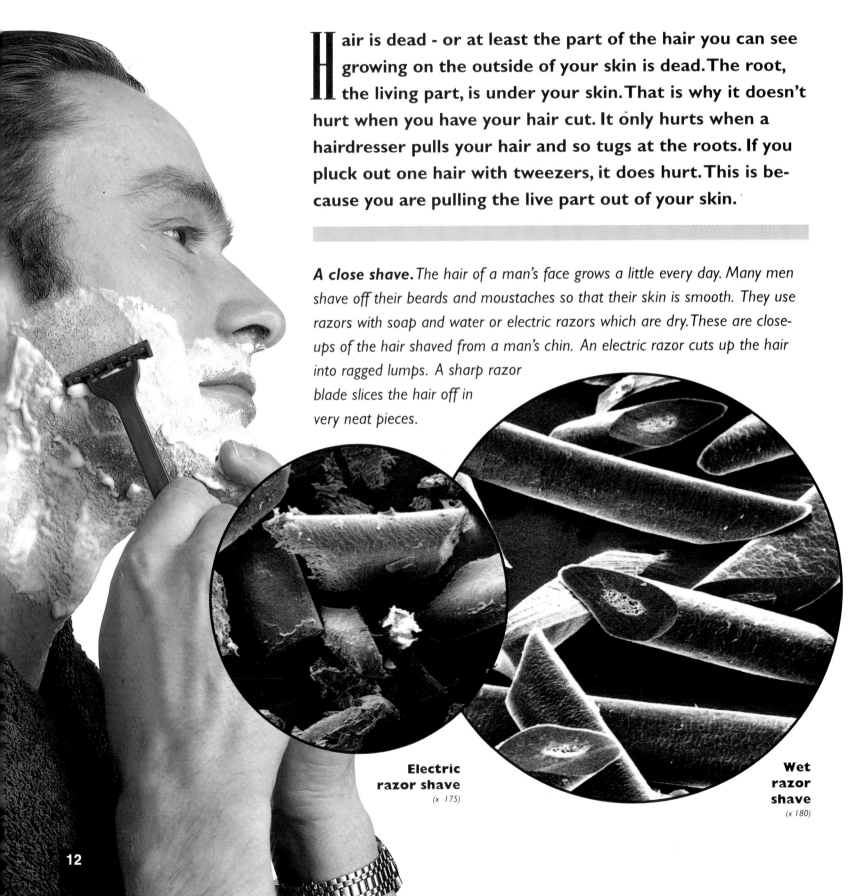

Hair is dead - or at least the part of the hair you can see growing on the outside of your skin is dead. The root, the living part, is under your skin. That is why it doesn't hurt when you have your hair cut. It only hurts when a hairdresser pulls your hair and so tugs at the roots. If you pluck out one hair with tweezers, it does hurt. This is because you are pulling the live part out of your skin.

A close shave. The hair of a man's face grows a little every day. Many men shave off their beards and moustaches so that their skin is smooth. They use razors with soap and water or electric razors which are dry. These are close-ups of the hair shaved from a man's chin. An electric razor cuts up the hair into ragged lumps. A sharp razor blade slices the hair off in very neat pieces.

Electric razor shave
(x 175)

Wet razor shave
(x 180)

Dirty hair
(x 80)

Clean hair
(x 80)

The hair on your head gets quite dirty only a few days after washing. This hair was washed four days ago and is already coated with tiny pieces of skin and dust.

This hair has just been washed with shampoo and rinsed in water. It is very clean and smooth.

Getting the chop (above).
This is how the scissor-cut ends of your hair look after a visit to the hairdresser's. Hair is quite tough and hairdressers have to use very sharp scissors. They cut the hair so it lies flat or into different styles. Everyone gets the colour and texture of their hair from their parents.

Sticky spray

Hair spray is a lacquer, or varnish, which is usually sold in aerosol cans. People spray it on their hair to keep it in place or in a particular style when they have been to the hairdresser's. The spray comes out in tiny drops and dries very quickly. It coats the hairs and sticks them together.

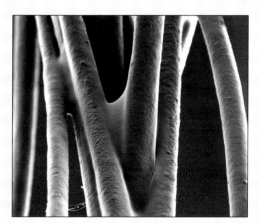

Hair spray on hair
(x 130)

A Question of Taste

Both your nose and your tongue help you to taste. Before you eat something, you usually smell it first. You can smell food cooking or you sniff at it before you take a bite. A smell gives you a good idea of what the food will taste like. A good food smell also makes your mouth water. The saliva, or spit, in your mouth helps you to digest your food while you chew it. Smelling is also part of tasting when you have a mouthful of food.

Smell sensitive skin
(x 15,500)

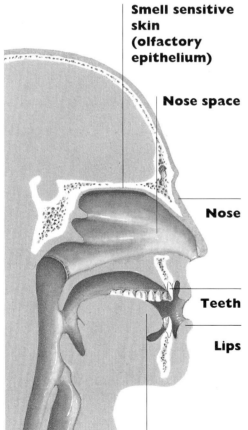

Smell sensitive skin (olfactory epithelium)

Nose space

Nose

Teeth

Lips

Tongue

On the scent. You breathe in and out of your nose all the time, but if you want to smell something, you sniff hard. This takes the air carrying the smells up your nose to a space at the top. Here the smells, which are tiny specks of chemicals, land on the special skin lining the top of the space. It is kept wet by a liquid called mucus. Mucus ends up on your handkerchief when you blow your nose.

The smell chemicals collect on the mucus and the special skin. In the skin, there are thousands of cells which are very sensitive to smell. They record the smell and send a message to your brain. Your brain then knows what the smell is.

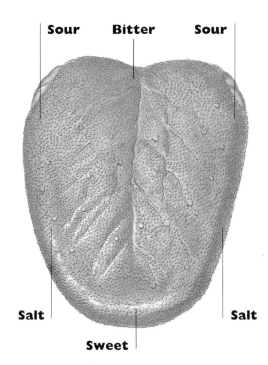

Sour Bitter Sour

Salt Salt

Sweet

These are the parts of your tongue which taste the different flavours of food. Your tongue also tells you if a food is hot or cold, rough or smooth.

Your tongue is very bumpy with tiny lumps called taste buds. They detect the flavour of food and send a message to your brain, telling you what it is.

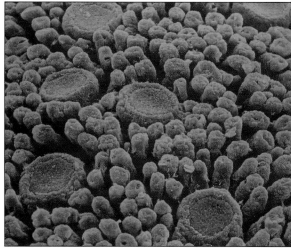

Surface of tongue
(x 100)

On the tip of your tongue. You taste food with your tongue and smell it at the same time. If you hold your nose while eating, you can't taste things as well. Different parts of your tongue are sensitive to different tastes. They will tell you if a food is bitter, sour, salty or sweet. Some foods are mixtures of them all.

You can check which part of your tongue responds to each taste by testing different places on its surface with salt, sugar and lemon juice or vinegar.

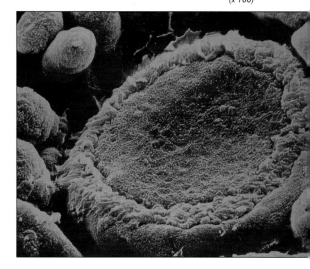

Taste bud
(x 2,000)

Careful brushwork

Your teeth have a hard coat on the outside, called enamel. Food on your teeth attacks the enamel and makes holes in it. This gives you toothache. Sticky, sugary food, sweets, sugary drinks and ices are the worst. Brushing your teeth properly cleans off the food and stops you getting toothache.

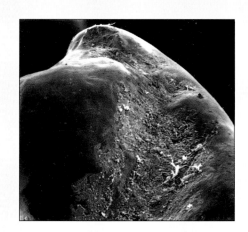

Tooth enamel
(x 25)

Vital Vision

Cornea
(x 1,300)

The tough, curved cover at the front of an eye, the cornea, is made of many tiny cells. It is transparent so that light can go through it into the eye.

Like little windows on the world, your eyes gather and process an endless stream of information about your surroundings every second that you are awake. Each eye is packed with many millions of special cells and lots of tiny, delicate muscles that help it to perform such a difficult task. Your eye lashes and eye lids protect your eyes and stop little bits of dirt and dust getting into them. Under your eye lids are special glands which make tears. The tears wash your eyes.

Seeing eye to eye. A human eye is a round ball, about 2.5cm across, full of a clear liquid. At the front is a transparent cover, called the cornea. The coloured part is called the iris. The black circle in the middle, the pupil, is a hole in the eye ball. Behind it is a lens which directs light going through the iris on to the back of the eye ball. Here are light-sensitive cells, packed into an area called the retina. They record the light and colours as pictures and send them as messages along a special nerve to the brain.

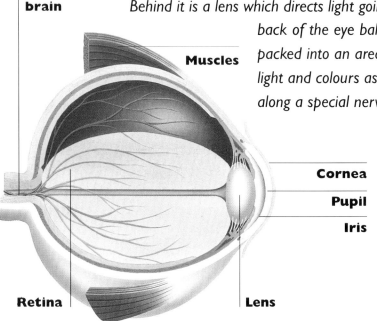

Nerve to brain

Muscles

Cornea

Pupil

Iris

Retina

Lens

Eyeball

DID YOU KNOW?

Your eyes don't "see" at all. They are like a camera which takes colour photographs of whatever you are looking at. They then pass messages, as electrical signals, to your brain which recognises the pictures.

Iris
(x 630)

Cells of the lens
(x 600)

The lens has lots of muscles around it. They change the shape of the lens to bend light from the things you are looking at and focus it on the back of your eye in a clear picture.

The iris is the coloured part of your eye. Muscles in it make the pupil bigger or smaller to control the amount of light going into your eye.

Retina
(x 850)

Fovea
(x 35)

In the picture. *Although the retina at the back of your eye is only as big as a postage stamp, it has about 127 million light-sensitive cells. About 120 million are called rods and are sensitive to light and dark. The others, called cones, are sensitive to colour. That is why it is difficult to see colours in very dim light. In the middle of the retina is a small spot called the fovea. Here there are only cones and they are very close together. There are lots of tiny blood vessels leading to the fovea.*

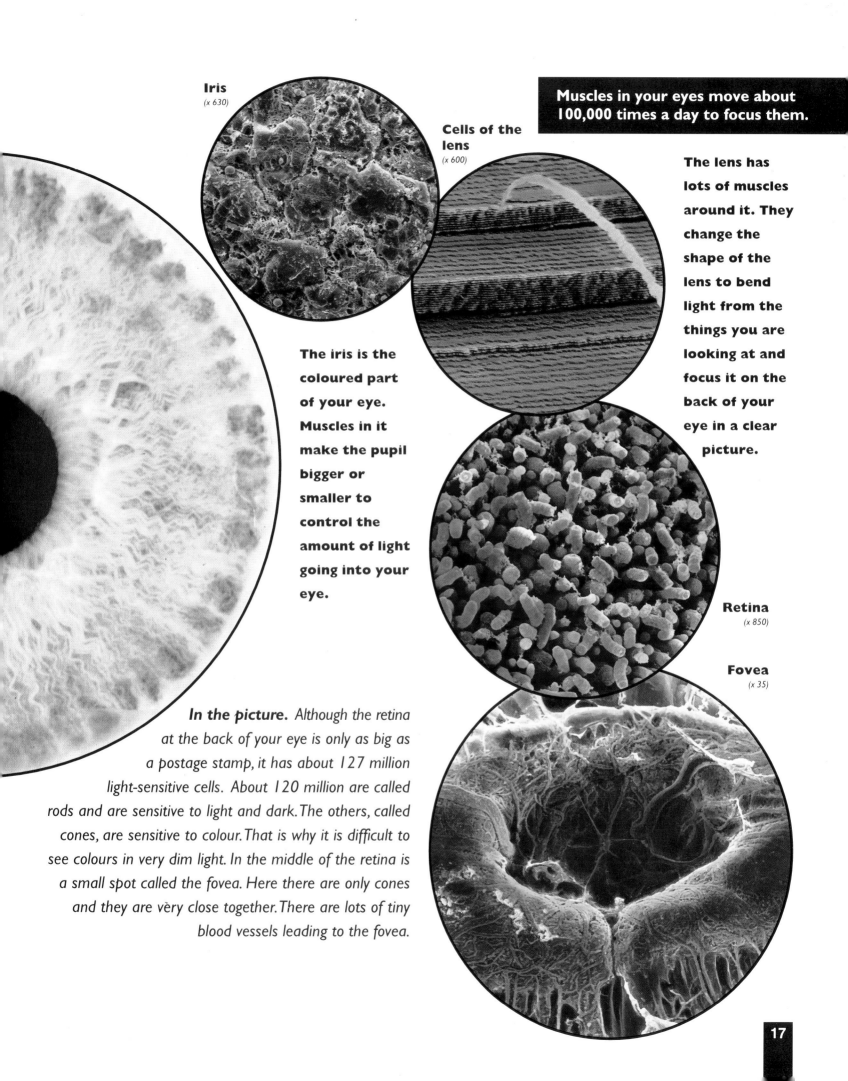

Playing by Ear

The ears on the outside of your head are just flaps of skin. You can't move them around much, in the way that animals can, but they do help you to hear sounds coming from all directions. Ears also play a part in keeping your body balanced as you move around. The important parts of your ears are inside your head.

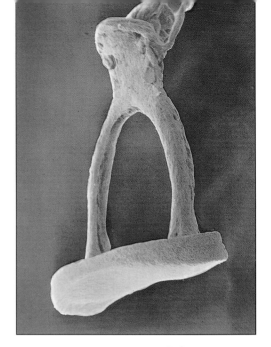

Stirrup bone
(x 40)

Sound system. Our ears have three parts. The first is the hole you can stick your finger in, called the ear canal. Across the end of it is a thin layer of skin, the ear drum. In the next part, the middle ear, are three small bones. There is also a tube to your throat. It controls the air pressure in your ear. The last part, the inner ear, has many cells which are sensitive to sound.

When you hear a sound or listen to music, it makes the air quiver, or vibrate. The quivering air reaches your ear drum and that vibrates. It passes the vibrations on to your middle ear which passes them on to your inner ear. Here the vibrations are turned into signals which go to your brain. Your brain then "hears" the sound or music.

The tiny stirrup bone in your middle ear gets its name from its shape. It is just like a stirrup used in horse riding. This bone receives sound vibrations from the ear drum and passes them on.

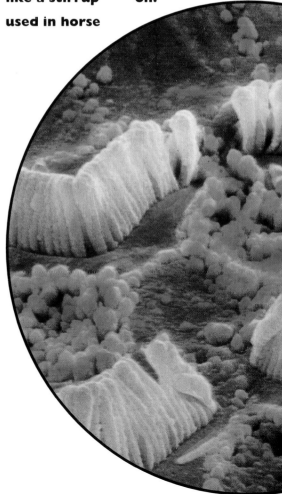

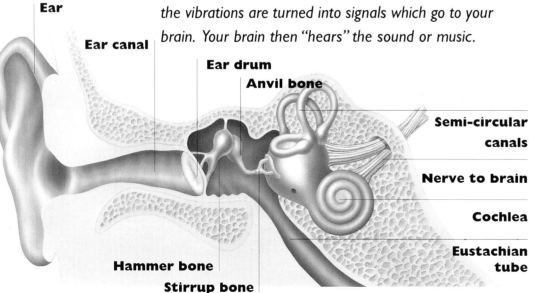

Ear

Ear canal

Ear drum

Anvil bone

Semi-circular canals

Nerve to brain

Cochlea

Eustachian tube

Hammer bone

Stirrup bone

Pressure cells in inner ear
(x 5,000)

Sound-carrying cells in inner ear
(x 6,000)

Striking a balance. Your ears let you hear sounds but they also help you to keep your balance. They tell you if you are upright or standing on your head. They tell you which position your head is in and when you turn it around.

In your inner ear are tubes full of liquid. Special cells in the liquid record the movements of your head and send messages to your brain.
Next to the tubes are tiny cells which are sensitive to pressure. They send messages to your brain which is then able to work out the position you are in.

Your body's smallest muscle is in your ear. It is only about 1mm long.

Life Support

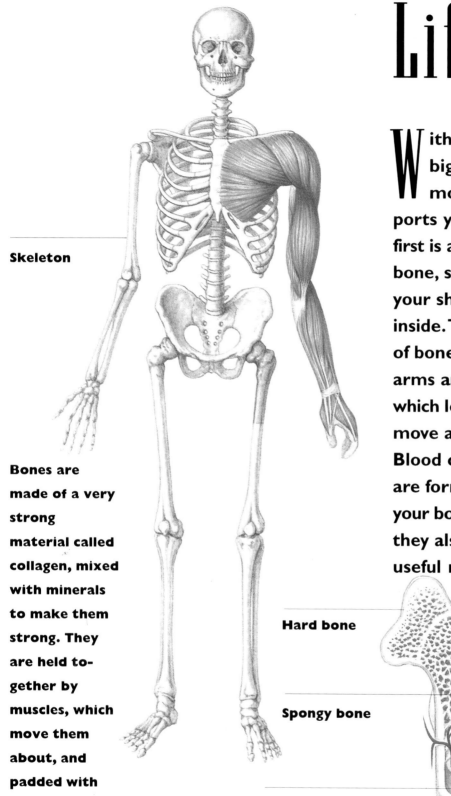

Skeleton

Bones are made of a very strong material called collagen, mixed with minerals to make them strong. They are held together by muscles, which move them about, and padded with gristle.

Without your bones, you would be a big, squashy bag of skin that couldn't move. Your skeleton holds up and supports your body. It has two main parts. The first is a frame, made up of your skull, backbone, shoulders, chest and hips. It gives you your shape and protects the delicate parts inside. The second group of bones are your arms and legs which let you move about. Blood cells are formed in your bones and they also store useful minerals.

Spongy bone

Hard bone

Spongy bone

Red marrow

Bone marrow produces 5 billion new blood cells a day, replacing the ones that die after 120 days.

DID YOU KNOW?

When a baby is born, it has over 800 bones. As it grows, some of the bones in its skull and other bones join together. By the time it is an adult, it has 206 bones. About half of them are in its hands and feet.

Close to the bone. *A human thigh bone is thick and hard on the outside. Inside, at each end, is a network of fine bone, called spongy bone. This makes the bone strong but light, able to support the body and to move about.*

There are lots of spaces between the tiny rods of bone. These are filled with soft red bone marrow where new red blood cells are made. Some white blood cells are made here as well. Some bone marrow also stores yellow fat which can be used when the body needs it.

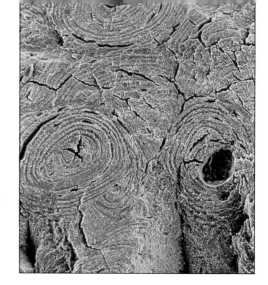

Compact bone
(x 140)

Blood vessels go through channels in the bone. Cells move between the blood and the bone, bringing the bone the things it needs to grow and renew itself, and taking away the waste material.

Spongy bone
(x 65)

Compact bone is the thick, strong, outer layer of bone. This cross-section of a thigh bone shows the rings of bone with blood vessels and nerves in the middle.

The blood carries the minerals, phosphorous and calcium, to the bones. But the bones give them up if the body needs the minerals somewhere else.

Muscle power. *Most muscles in the body are attached to the bones and move them about. These muscles, called skeletal muscles, are bundles of fibres which are made of overlapping threads of protein. There are two threads, one thick and one thin.*

Signals sent by the brain along the nerves cause chemical reactions in each muscle fibre. These reactions make the protein threads in the fibres move closer together. This shortens the muscle and makes it move.

Fibril
(x 1,200)

This is the tiniest fibre that can be separated from a bundle of muscle.

Muscle

Bundle of fibres

Fibril

Taking Air

All day, and all night when you are asleep, you are breathing in and out. Most of the time you don't notice that your chest is moving gently up and down and that your lungs are pumping away, taking in air. Controlled by your brain, the muscles of your body work automatically so that you can breathe without having to think about it. You also use the air in your lungs to breathe out when you speak, sing or shout, or blow up a balloon.

Hairs, or cilia, in breathing tubes
(x 1,000)

The tubes leading to your lungs are lined with tiny hairs, called cilia. They help to clean the air going into your lungs, collecting dust and other tiny pieces of rubbish.

Breathtaking. When you take a deep breath, air goes in through your mouth or nose and down your wind pipe. The end of your wind pipe divides into two tubes which lead to your two lungs. The two tubes divide into smaller tubes which eventually lead to tiny air bags, each one surrounded by minute blood vessels.

Oxygen in the air goes through the walls of the thousands of tiny air bags and into the blood vessels. Your heart pumps the blood around your body, carrying the oxygen to where it is used to make energy. This process of making energy produces carbon dioxide which goes into the blood, is carried back to your lungs and is breathed out.

Tiny air bags in lungs
(x 150)

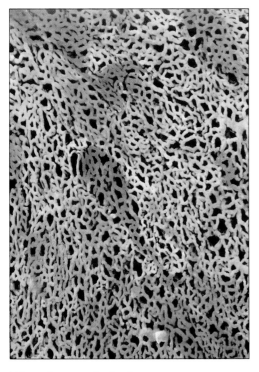

Blood vessels in lungs
(x 160)

The walls of the tiny air bags in your lungs are a mass of tiny blood vessels. If they were all put in a line, they would reach over half way around the world.

Your wind pipe leads down to your two lungs. It divides into two and then into many more tubes. These go to the thousands of tiny air bags, called alveoli.

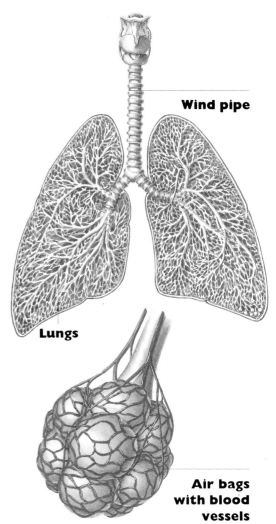

Wind pipe

Lungs

Air bags with blood vessels

Pump it up. The muscles between your ribs move them up and down to pump air in and out of your lungs. When you take a deep breath, you can feel your chest swell outwards and grow bigger. There is also a very large muscle just under your ribs, above your stomach, called the diaphragm. This moves down to draw air into your lungs and then up again to push the air out.

When you are sitting down or are asleep, you breathe in and out about 18 times a minute. When you are running or playing games, you need more energy. Special chemicals in your blood send messages to your brain. Your brain sends messages to your muscles and you breathe more quickly or pant. Your lungs take in more air, passing more oxygen to your body and making the energy you need.

DID YOU KNOW?

Your lungs hold enough air to fill a large party balloon. Every time you breathe in, you take in about enough air to fill two cups, which you breathe out again. Even when you breathe out very hard, though, there is still lots of air left in your lungs.

A man running fast breathes in over 15 buckets of air a minute.

Food Factory

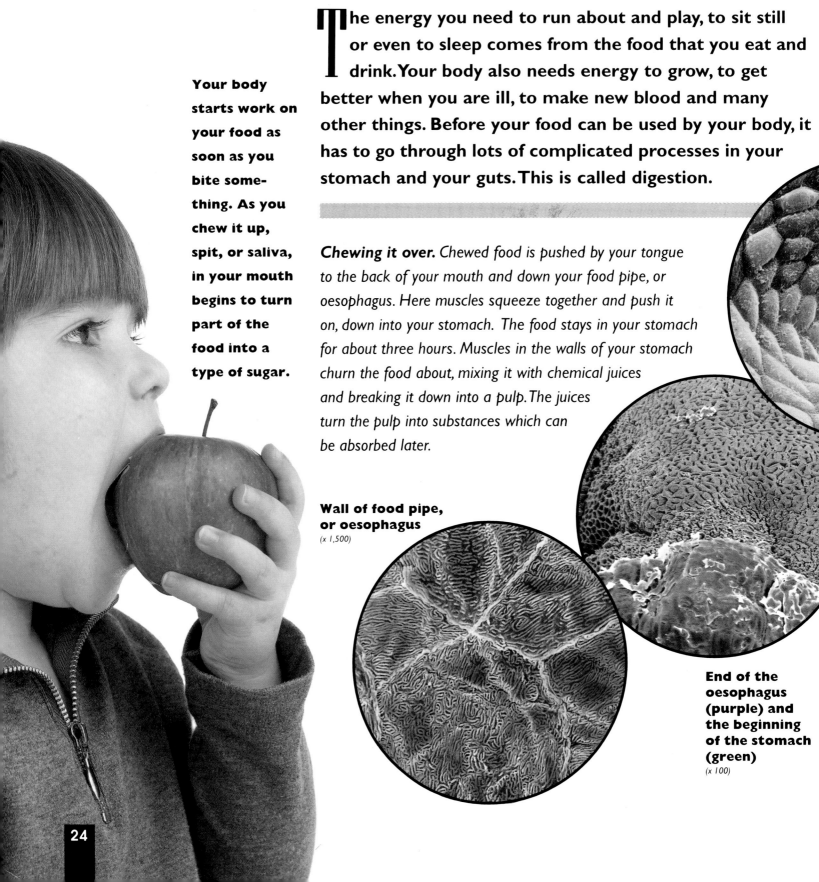

The energy you need to run about and play, to sit still or even to sleep comes from the food that you eat and drink. Your body also needs energy to grow, to get better when you are ill, to make new blood and many other things. Before your food can be used by your body, it has to go through lots of complicated processes in your stomach and your guts. This is called digestion.

Your body starts work on your food as soon as you bite something. As you chew it up, spit, or saliva, in your mouth begins to turn part of the food into a type of sugar.

Chewing it over. Chewed food is pushed by your tongue to the back of your mouth and down your food pipe, or oesophagus. Here muscles squeeze together and push it on, down into your stomach. The food stays in your stomach for about three hours. Muscles in the walls of your stomach churn the food about, mixing it with chemical juices and breaking it down into a pulp. The juices turn the pulp into substances which can be absorbed later.

Wall of food pipe, or oesophagus
(x 1,500)

End of the oesophagus (purple) and the beginning of the stomach (green)
(x 100)

24

Villi at the end of the small intestine wave about in the food pulp, taking the digested parts into the blood stream.

Villi
(x 80)

If your small intestine was straightened out, it would be nearly 7 metres long.

Wall of small intestine where it joins large intestine
(x 120)

Facts to digest. Food pulp in your stomach moves, a little at a time, into your small intestine. This is a very long tube which is coiled up below your stomach. More juices from glands and the walls mix with the pulp, breaking it down, or digesting it. The small intestine is lined with thousands of wrinkles like tiny fingers, called villi. The digested food goes through the villi into the blood stream. What is left of the food, the tough, woody parts that can't be digested, goes into the large intestine. It comes out of your body as waste.

Wall of stomach with gastric juice gland
(x 850)

These are the parts of your body which deal with the food you eat. The whole system is about 10m long and digestion takes about 24 hours from eating to going to the toilet.

Mouth

Tongue

Saliva, or spit, glands

Food pipe, or oesophagus

Stomach

Small intestine

Appendix

DID YOU KNOW?

The muscles in your stomach sometimes keep moving even when all the food has passed on to your small intestine and it is empty. This gives you hunger pains in your stomach. Hunger pains stop as soon as you eat something.

All in the Blood

Blood is your body's transport system. It takes food to every part of the body, except the nails, hair and front of the eyes. It carries oxygen from the air breathed in by the lungs and takes the waste gas back to be breathed out. Blood also helps to keep the body at just the right temperature, fights off germs and diseases and stops wounds from bleeding.

DID YOU KNOW?

You have blood vessels, some about 2cm across and some as thin as a hair, in almost every part of your body. Added together, you have nearly 100,000km of blood vessels. That is long enough to go more than twice around the Earth.

Blood building blocks. Human blood is made up of tiny red and white cells, blood platelets and a liquid called plasma. The plasma has many chemicals as well as food substances in it. There are a huge number of round red cells, which make blood look red. They carry oxygen from the lungs around the body and take back waste gas, carbon dioxide. There are less white cells. They defend the body against infections from cuts and wounds. The blood platelets make the blood clot and stop wounds from bleeding.

Red cell
(x 8,000)

White cell
(x 8,000)

Blood platelet
(x 8,000)

A healthy human being has about 5 litres of blood.

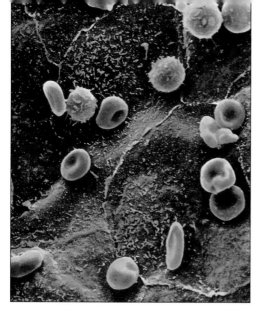

Red cells inside heart
(x 1,000)

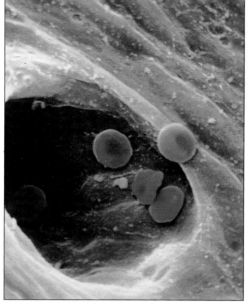

Red cells moving from large artery into small one
(x 1,000)

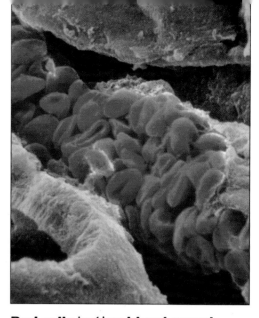

Red cells in tiny blood vessel
(x 1,000)

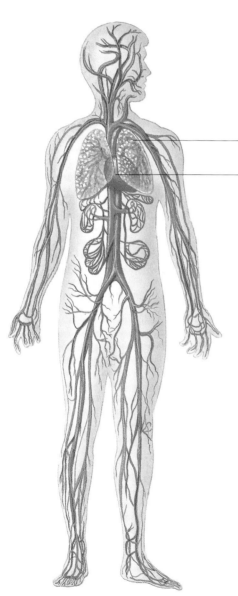

Lung

Heart

Circulation of blood

Essentials on stream. *Blood is pumped around the body by the heart. The heart, which is about the size of a man's fist, is made of special muscles. The blood picks up oxygen from the lungs and carries it along thick blood vessels, called arteries. These divide into smaller and smaller ones, right down to tiny capillaries. After the blood has delivered its oxygen, it picks up carbon dioxide from the body and returns it along veins to the lungs, where it collects more oxygen. Blood also delivers chemicals and food substances from the stomach and small intestine to all parts of the body and takes away waste.*

Patching up

When you cut your skin, blood may ooze from the wound and germs can enter your body. To stop this happening, the platelets in your blood work together with a special substance called fibrin (seen here on a red blood cell) to make the blood in the wound clot and form a scab.

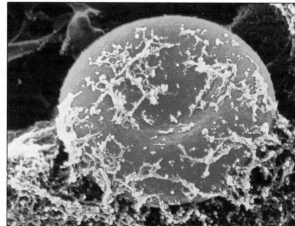

Red blood cell covered with fibrin
(x 6,000)

Getting the Message

Nervous system

Brain

Spinal cord

Nerves

A complicated electrical circuit inside your body? Believe it or not, that is exactly what your nervous system really is. It is made up of your nerves, your brain and the spinal column in your backbone. This system keeps you alive by telling you what is going on outside as well as inside your body. It works by electricity which travels through billions of nerve cells, passing on information and instructions.

Plenty of nerve. There are three main types of nerve cells in your body. One type receives information from your senses, which tell you about the things you smell, taste, see, hear and feel, such as pain and heat. They send the information on to your brain and other parts of your nervous system.

The second type of nerve cells carry messages from your nervous system to your muscles and glands. The messages tell them what to do. They keep your heart beating, your lungs breathing and all the other parts of your body working. The third type are the linking ones which pass the messages from one cell to the next cell by electrical impulses.

Nerves reach all parts of your body. The most important ones go to your brain which receives information and sends back messages.

Running up inside your backbone is your spinal cord. It is made up of many bundles of nerve cells which carry messages to and from your brain.

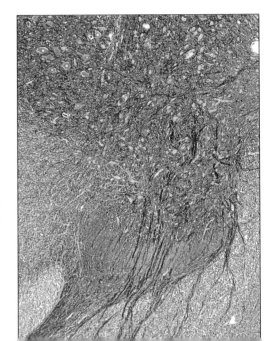

Spinal cord
(x 80)

Nerve centre. *In part of your brain are masses of nerve cells. Some receive messages from the nervous system and some send out messages. The simplest reaction to a message sent along your nervous system is one you do not think about. If you touch something very hot, you quickly move your hand away. The nerves in your skin on your fingers send a message to your nervous system, telling it that your fingers are getting very hot. It sends a message to your muscles and your hand quickly moves away from the heat and stops your fingers from being burnt. This is called a reflex action.*

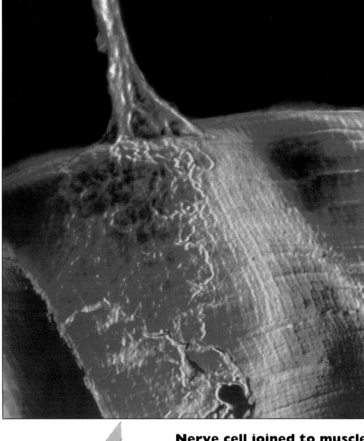

Nerve cell joined to muscle
(x 700)

Bundles of linking cells

Nerve cell

Muscles

When a message from your fingers reaches the cells joined to muscles in your arm, they contract. This pulls your hand quickly away from the heat.

Brain nerve cells
(x 230)

When you sneeze, the air comes out of your lungs at over 150kph. That is faster than a real hurricane.

Aa-tishoo!

Sneezing is a reflex action. When tiny pieces of something irritating, such as dust or pepper, settle on the nerve endings in your nose, it makes you take a deep breath. The top of your wind pipe closes and the pressure builds up in your lungs. Your wind pipe then opens and the air explodes out in a sneeze, blowing the dust or pepper out of your nose.

A New Life

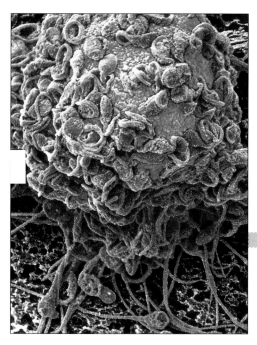

Sperm on egg
(x 700)

Every human baby starts as a tiny egg inside its mother. But the egg only grows and develops into a baby after a sperm from the father has got into the egg and fertilized it. The sperm and the egg become one cell which gets everything - the colour of its skin, hair and eyes, and all the other things that are special about one human being - from its father and mother. The father's sperm decides what sex the baby will be.

Long division. Just over a day after fertilization, the egg divides into two cells. During the next few days, it divides into more cells. It is then only about the size of an apple pip. It moves to the part of the mother's body where it will stay and grow for the next nine months.

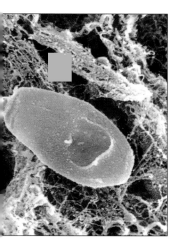

Sperm
(x 4,500)

Sperm are like tiny tadpoles with long tails. Hundreds of sperm swarm over an egg, trying to get in. As soon as one gets inside, the skin of the egg thickens to keep all the others out and they soon die.

After about six days, it links up to its mother's blood supply by a special cord and gets food and oxygen from her blood. Its heart starts beating after about three weeks. As it grows, a skin develops around it and it floats in a bag of liquid which protects it. After a few weeks, this tiny blob of life, called an embryo, has a head, brain and spine.

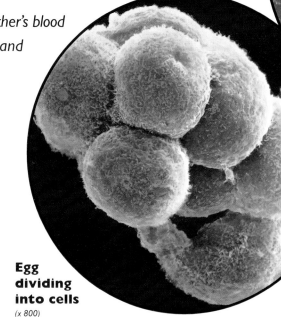

Egg dividing into cells
(x 800)

After about six months an embryo can hear and even jumps at very sudden, loud noises.

At about seven weeks, the embryo is about the size of a walnut. Its legs have grown and you can see its toes.

Embryo at four months

Embryo at seven weeks

Embryo at five weeks

After about five weeks, the embryo's head starts to take shape. The dark spot is an eye. The arms and legs are still just buds and the red blob is its heart.

Growth spurt. At about four months, the embryo is growing very quickly. The arms and hands are developing faster than the legs and feet. The ears have grown and eyes are in position but they do not yet have eyelids.

After another three months, the embryo weighs about 1kg. It is now moving about, kicking its legs and waving its arms.

After nine months, the baby weighs over 2kg. Just before it is born, the bag of special liquid breaks. As soon the baby is born, it starts to breathe and the cord which joins it to its mother is cut. It is now a fully developed human baby.

Body at War

Many of the diseases which make people ill are caused by tiny bacteria and viruses. They get into our bodies through cuts and scratches, through insect bites, through our mouths and noses when we breathe in, and in the food we eat. A healthy body can often fight off most diseases, but sometimes a person needs medicine or surgery to help them get well again.

'Flu bacteria
(x 16,000)

These four white cells are attacking a cancer tumour. They are a special part of the blood which help to fight diseases.

Meningitis bacteria
(x 10,000)

White blood cells attacking tumour
(x 4,500)

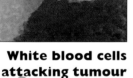

Viruses cause common diseases such as colds and 'flu for which there is no known cure.

No defence. This white blood cell has been invaded by the HIV virus. This virus causes the AIDS disease. The virus, the green dots, takes over the cell and destroys it. Then it multiplies and spreads to more cells, killing them.

As more and more cells are destroyed, the person's body cannot fight off infections and may become ill with a disease such as pneumonia.

HIV virus on white blood cell
(x 7,000)

The long bac-teria cause a type of 'flu in young children. The round ones cause an infection of the lining of the brain, called meningitis.

Tuberculosis bacteria (x 5,000)

Pneumonia bacteria (x 12,000)

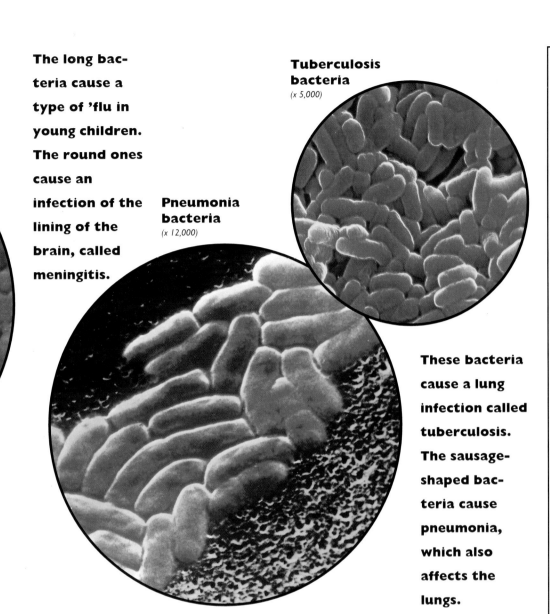

These bacteria cause a lung infection called tuberculosis. The sausage-shaped bac-teria cause pneumonia, which also affects the lungs.

Germ warfare. Many diseases today are controlled by a special process called inoculation. Each person (usually a child) is injected with some of the germs that actually cause the disease. These germs are specially treated so that they are either dead or very weak. The person's defence system can easily fight off the weak germs. At the same time, his or her body builds up a resistance to that particular disease. If the same person later comes into contact with germs of the real disease, he or she can fight them off without getting ill. People are inoculated against diseases such as smallpox, diphtheria, whooping cough and tuberculosis.

Dainty stitchwork

Surgery is used to cure some diseases. In microsurgery, surgeons watch what they are doing through a micro-scope and use tiny, very delicate instruments. A needle may be only as long as this -. Here a surgeon is operating on a patient's eye. A close-up of the eye shows up on a television screen.

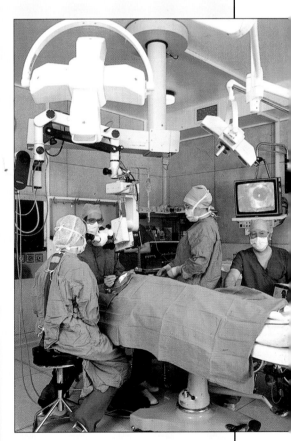

Microsurgery

People Pests

Fungus of athlete's foot
(x 2,000)

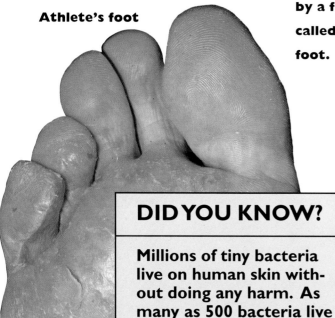

Athlete's foot

H uman beings sometimes have creatures living on them. Some are just visitors which come for a meal but some spend their whole lives on a human body. They can make someone feel itchy and want to scratch. Many do not cause real illness but some of the visitors can carry diseases which they pick up from one person and then give to another.

The sore, cracked skin on this human foot is caused by a fungus, called athlete's foot.

Fungus foot (left). Athlete's foot is an infection caused by a fungus which can be picked up very easily in warm, damp places, such as swimming pools. It is called athlete's foot because athletes, whose feet are often hot and sweaty, commonly suffer from it. Some people have the infection on their feet so mildly that they don't know it is there. If the infection is serious, the skin of the feet becomes scaly and blistered, particularly between the toes, and it can be very itchy.

Keeping the feet dry, well dusted with talcum powder and clean usually gets rid of the fungus. It can be very difficult to get rid of, though, if the toenails are infected. In such cases, a doctor will prescribe a special cream which kills the fungus off completely.

DID YOU KNOW?

Millions of tiny bacteria live on human skin without doing any harm. As many as 500 bacteria live on a dot the size of a full stop on the skin of a human armpit where it is warm and damp.

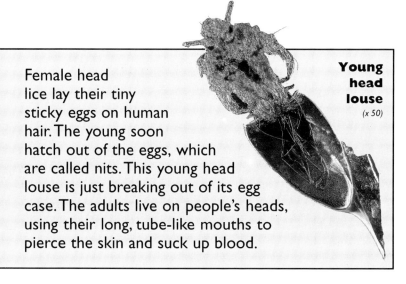

Female head lice lay their tiny sticky eggs on human hair. The young soon hatch out of the eggs, which are called nits. This young head louse is just breaking out of its egg case. The adults live on people's heads, using their long, tube-like mouths to pierce the skin and suck up blood.

Young head louse
(x 50)

Body louse
(x 70)

Blood banquet. Female mosquitoes land on human skin and use their tube-like mouths to suck up blood. In hot climates, some mosquitoes carry thousands of tiny parasites, which cause the disease malaria. When a mosquito bites someone, the parasites go through the wound and into the blood. They rapidly multiply in the red blood cells. Every now and again, they burst out of the blood cells and the person has an attack of malaria.

This mosquito lives in cold, northern climates. It does not carry malaria, but its bite can cause a large, painful lump on a person's skin.

Body lice live in the seams and folds of people's clothes. They feed on the person's blood and make the skin sore and itchy. These lice may spread diseases.

Mosquito on skin

Head of mosquito
(x 25)

Every year, over 200 million people catch malaria and 2 million die of the disease.

Guess What?

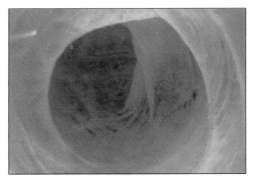

1. Tummy trouble - you could only explore this mysterious cave if someone gobbled you up!

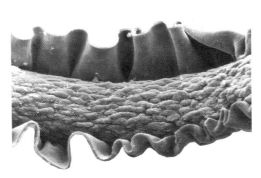

2. A snake shedding its skin? - you may get into a tangle with this, but luckily it's totally harmless.

3. Crowded wormhole - new yet already dead, these still grow so fast that they often need cutting.

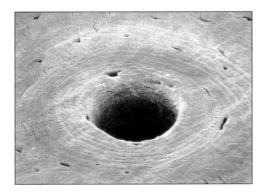

4. Hole in one - you'd feel a bit below par if you were unfortunate enough to break one of these.

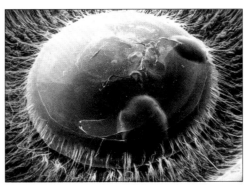

5. Gigantic jellyfish? - you're actually using two of these as you try to recognise this picture.

6. Carpenter's workshop - this stuff is certainly an essential part of your basic framework.

7. Pretty braid - don't be tempted, though, even a tiny snip would be very bad for your health.

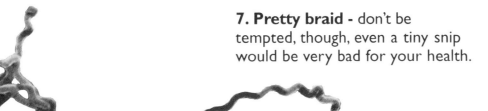

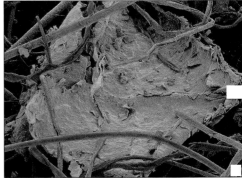

8. Party piece - a bit of wrapping paper covered with streamers? It wraps *you* up from head to foot.

1 inside of small intestine/**2** split human hair (x 265)/**3** hairs on scalp (x 600)/**4** part of compact bone (x 300)/**5** lens of eye from behind (x 14)/ **6** part of compact bone (x 1,200)/**7** type of bacteria that causes serious disease (x 21,000)/**8** skin flake in household dust (x 2,000)

GLOSSARY

Alveoli - thousands of tiny air bags in the lungs. Oxygen passes through the walls of the air bags into the blood vessels.

Antibiotics - chemicals produced by a mould or fungus that stop germs and bacteria in the body from growing and spreading.

Blood platelets - tiny cells in the blood that help it to clot.

Cilia - tiny hairs that line the tubes leading to the lungs. They help to clean the air going into your lungs. There are also cilia in your nose, which stimulate smell-sensitive cells to send messages to the brain.

Cornea - the tough, curved cover at the front of the eye. It is clear so that light can go through it into the eye.

Diaphragm - the large muscle just under your ribs. It moves down to draw air into your lungs and up again to push the air out.

Digestion - a series of processes that take place in your mouth, stomach and intestines to break food down into different substances. Your body then uses these to make energy.

Ear drum - the thin layer of skin in the ear that vibrates when sound waves reach it. The ear drum passes the vibrations on to other parts of the ear.

Embryo - the early stage of development of a human baby inside its mother.

Fovea - a small spot in the middle of the retina of the eye. It contains masses of colour-sensitive cells that help you to see things in great detail.

Iris - the coloured part of the eye. Its muscles alter the size of the pupil and control the amount of light going into the eye.

Keratin - the tough material that makes hair and nails.

Lens - the rounded transparent structure behind the iris of the eye which helps you to focus.

Microsurgery - a form of medicine in which the surgeon uses a microscope and tiny, very delicate instruments to repair damaged or diseased tissue.

Nerve cells - cells throughout the body that carry or transmit messages to and from the brain.

Nervous system - the combination of nerves, brain and the spinal cord in the backbone that passes information and instructions around the body to keep it working.

Pupil - the black circle in the middle of the eye. It is a hole in the eyeball, allowing light to go into the eye.

Red blood cells - cells in the blood that carry oxygen from the lungs to the rest of the body. They also take back waste gas.

Retina - the area at the back of the eye which is packed with special light-sensitive cells. The retina detects light and colours, records them as pictures and sends them as messages to the brain.

Skeleton - the framework of bones that supports your body and protects the delicate parts inside.

Skin - the tough, waterproof cover all over your body. Skin is full of blood vessels and nerves. It also contains hair roots and sweat glands.

Spinal cord - bundles of nerve cells running up inside the backbone, which carry messages to and from your brain.

Taste buds - cells on your tongue that detect the flavour of food and send a message to the brain telling you what each taste is.

Villi - tiny projections like fingers that line the small intestine. The villi help digested food to be absorbed into the blood stream.

White blood cells - cells in the blood that help to protect the body from disease and to repair parts that are damaged.

INDEX

A

AIDS 32
alveoli (wind bags) 22
artery 27
athlete's foot 34

B

bacteria 34, 36
    flu 32
    Leptospira 36
    meningitis 32
    pneumonia 33
    tuberculosis 33
blood 21, 35
    cells 20, 21, 26, 32, 35
    circulation 22, 27
    clotting 26, 27
    stream 25, 26-27
    vessels 8, 21, 23, 26
blood-sucking insects 35
body heat 8, 9
body lice 35
bone, compact 21, 36
    marrow 20, 21
    spongy 21
    stirrup 18
    thigh 21
bones 20-21
brain 28
breathing 22-23

C

cancer tumour 32
carbon dioxide 22, 26
cell division 30
cilia 22
collagen 20
compact bone 21, 36
cornea 16

D

diaphragm 23
digestion 14, 24-25
disease 32-33

E

ears 18, 19
    canal 18
    drum 18
    inner 18
    middle 18
eating 24-25
embryo 30, 31
energy 22, 23, 24
eye 16-17, 26
    cornea 16
    eyeball 16-17
    fovea 16, 17
    iris 16
    lens 16, 36
    muscles 16, 17
    pupil 16
    retina 17
eye surgery 33

F

fertilization 30
fingerprints 6
fingertips 6-7, 10
food pipe (oesophagus) 24
food pulp 24-25
fovea 16, 17
fungus 34

G

gastric gland 25
gastric juices 25
glands 7, 28

H

hair 7, 8, 10-11, 26, 35, 36
    colour 13
    root 10
    tip 11
    damaged 10
hairspray 13
hands 6
head lice 34
hearing 18-19

heart 22, 27, 28
HIV virus 32
hunger pains 25

I

inner ear 18
inoculation 33
insect bites 32
intestine, large 25
    small 25, 36
iris 16

K

keratin 7, 11

L

large intestine 25
lens 16
lips 10
liver 25
lungs 22, 23, 27, 28, 29, 33

M

malaria 35
microscope 4
    electron 4
    light 4
microsurgery 33
middle ear 18
mucus 14
muscle fibre 21
muscles 20, 21, 22, 23, 28, 29

N

nails 6, 7, 8-9, 11, 26
nerve cells 28, 29
nerve endings 6, 8
nerves 28
nervous system 28-29
nose 14, 29

O

oesophagus (food pipe) 24
oxygen 22, 26

P

pain 8
palms 6, 9, 10
plasma 26
platelets 26
pupil 16

R

razor, electric 12
        wet 12
red blood cells 26, 35
reflex action 29
retina 17

S

saliva 14, 24
senses 28, 29, 30
shaving 12

skeleton 20-21
skin 7, 8-9, 34, 35, 36
small intestine 25, 36
smell 14-15
sneezing 29
sperm 30
spinal column 28
spongy bone 21
stirrup bone 18
stomach 24-25
sweat 8-9
        glands 7
        pore 9

T

taste 14-15
        buds 15
thigh bone 21

toes 10
tongue 15, 24, 25
tooth brushing 15
        enamel 15
toothache 15
touch 6, 8, 29
trachea (windpipe) 23
tuberculosis bacteria 33
twins 31

V

veins 27
villi 25

W

white blood cells 26, 32
wind bags (alveoli) 22
wind pipe (trachea) 23, 29

ACKNOWLEDGEMENTS

The authors and publishers would like to thank Andrew Syred of Microscopix, Liz Hirst at the National Insitute of Medical Research and Steve Gorton for their assistance in the preparation of this book, as well as the other photographers and organisations listed below for their kind permission to reproduce the following photographs:

Dr Tony Brain; 6 top right, 7 top right, 10 left of centre, 13 bottom right, 15 bottom right, 22 top right, 35 top right, back cover right of centre

Steve Gorton; 6-7, 9 bottom, 10 bottom, 12 left, 13 right, 14-15 bottom, 19 left, 22 bottom left, 24 bottom left, 29 bottom left, 31 bottom right

The Natural History Museum, London; 36 above centre

Science Photo Library; 13 top left and left of centre /**Biophoto Associates**; 34 top /**Dr Tony Brain**; 11 left of centre, 13 above centre /**Jeremy Burgess**; 7 left of centre and right of centre, 9 top right and right of centre /**CNRI**; 3 right of centre, 10 right of centre, 18 top right, 21 top right and bottom right, 22-23 bottom, 27 top right, 28-29 centre, 32 top right and centre, 33 above centre and left, 36 bottom left /**A B Dowsett**; 27 bottom right /**Ralph Eagle**; front cover centre, 16-17 centre, 36 centre /**Stevie Grand**; 4 bottom left /**Manfred Kage**; 35 centre and 36 top left /**Dr Andrejs Liepins**; 32 left of centre /**Dr P Marazzi**; 34 bottom /**Professor P Motta/Dept of Anatomy/University of "La Sapienza"/Rome**; 3 left, 5 left and right, 8-9 top, 16 top left, 17 top left, top right, right of centre and bottom right, 18-19 bottom, 19 top right, 20-21, 23 top left, 24 below centre and bottom right, 25 top left and top right, 27 top left and above centre, 30 bottom left, 36 left of centre and right of centre, back cover top left /**Professors P M Motta, K R Porter and P M Andrews**; 24-25 centre /**Professors P M Motta and J van Blerkon**; 30 bottom right /**NASA**; 1, 6 centre /**NIBSC**; 26, 32 bottom left / **Claude Nuridsany and Marie Perennou**; 20 right /**OMIKRON**; 3 bottom right, 15 top right and right of centre /**Petit Format/Nestle**; 30-31 centre, 31 centre and top right, back cover bottom left /**J C Revy**; 35 top left /**St Bartholomew's Hospital**; 33 bottom right /**David Scharf**; 10-11 centre, 30 top left, 36 top right and bottom right /**SECCHI-LECAQUE/ROUSSEL-UCLAF/CNRI**; 14 top right, 29 top right /**Jeremy Trew**; 4 top left

Andrew Syred/Microscopix; 4 top right, right of centre, bottom right and below centre, 11 top left and right, 12 below centre and right, 28 bottom right, 35 bottom right

ZEFA; front cover left and right

ILLUSTRATORS:

Richard Coombes 20, 21, 27 left, 28
Jane Gedye 6, 13, 15 bottom left, 27 bottom centre, 29 bottom right, 33, 34
Paul Richardson 8, 14, 15 top left, 23, 25
Ed Stuart 5 centre, 16, 18, 29 centre